THE SONGS OF JULE STYNE

A special thanks to Frank Military.

WITHDRAWN

FAUQUIER COUNTY PUBLIC LIBRARY
1000169554

Hal Leonard Publishing Corporation
7777 West Bluemound Road P.O. Box 13819 Milwaukee, WI 53213

Copyright © 1989 HAL LEONARD PUBLISHING CORPORATION
International Copyright Secured   ALL RIGHTS RESERVED   Printed in the U.S.A.
For all works contained herein:
Unauthorized copying, arranging, adapting, recording or public performance is an infringement of copyright.
Infringers are liable under the law.

FAUQUIER COUNTY PUBLIC LIBRARY
11 Winchester Street
Warrenton, VA 22186

752.8154
STY

C O N T

Page	Title	Show
18	All I Need Is The Girl	*Gypsy*
26	As Long As There's Music	*Step Lively*
21	Be A Santa	*Subways Are For Sleeping*
30	Bye Bye Baby	*Gentlemen Prefer Blondes*
38	Can't You Just See Yourself?	*High Button Shoes*
34	Charm Of You, The	*Anchor's Aweigh*
36	Christmas Waltz, The	
43	Come Out, Come Out, Wherever You Are	*Step Lively*
48	Comes Once In A Lifetime	*Subways Are For Sleeping*
51	Diamonds Are A Girl's Best Friend	*Gentlemen Prefer Blondes*
54	Don't Rain On My Parade	*Funny Girl*
59	Ev'ry Street's A Boulevard (In Old New York)	*Hazel Flag*
64	Everything's Coming Up Roses	*Gypsy*
72	Five Minutes More	
69	Funny Girl	*Funny Girl*
74	Guess I'll Hang My Tears Out To Dry	*Glad To See You*
80	Hey Look, No Cryin'	
78	How Do You Speak To An Angel	*Hazel Flag*
85	I Believe	*It Happened In Brooklyn*
100	I Don't Want To Walk Without You Baby	*Sweater Girl*
88	I Fall In Love Too Easily	*Anchor's Aweigh*
90	I Still Get Jealous	*High Button Shoes*
92	I'll Walk Alone	*Follow The Boys*
96	I'm Glad I Waited For You	*Tars And Spars*
98	I've Heard That Song Before	*Youth On Parade*
103	Individual Thing	*Prettybelle*
106	It's Been A Long, Long Time	
108	It's Magic	*Romance On The High Seas*
110	It's The Same Old Dream	*It Happened In Brooklyn*
116	It's You Or No One	*Romance On The High Seas*
118	Just In Time	*Bells Are Ringing*

E N T S

113	Killing Time	
122	Let It Snow! Let It Snow! Let It Snow!	
124	Let Me Entertain You	*Gypsy*
130	Let's See What Happens	*Darling Of The Day*
134	Little Girl From Little Rock	*Gentlemen Prefer Blondes*
127	Long Before I Knew You	*Bells Are Ringing*
138	Make Someone Happy	*Do Re Mi*
141	Music That Makes Me Dance	*Funny Girl*
146	My Own Morning	*Hallelujah Baby*
150	Never Never Land	*Peter Pan*
156	On A Sunday By The Sea	*High Button Shoes*
158	Papa, Won't You Dance With Me?	*High Button Shoes*
153	The Party's Over	*Bells Are Ringing*
162	People	*Funny Girl*
166	Ride On A Rainbow, A	*Ruggles Of Redgap*
169	Saturday Night Is The Loneliest Night Of The Week	
174	Small World	*Gypsy*
178	Some Other Time	*Step Lively*
186	Some People	*Gypsy*
183	(Doin' It For) Sugar	*Sugar*
190	Things We Did Last Summer, The	
193	Three Coins In The Fountain	*Three Coins In The Fountain*
196	Time After Time	*It Happened In Brooklyn*
200	To A Small Degree	*Prettybelle*
206	Together Wherever We Go	*Gypsy*
210	What Makes The Sunset	*Anchor's Aweigh*
203	Who Are You Now	*Funny Girl*
214	You'll Never Get Away From Me	*Gypsy*
217	You're My Girl	*High Button Shoes*
220	You Are Woman, I Am Man	*Funny Girl*

BIOGRAPHY

COMPOSER   MUSIC PUBLISHER   PRODUCER

b. London, Eng., December 31, 1905. ASCAP 1931. Of musical parentage.

Education: began study of music in Chicago at eight.

Studied piano, composition, and theory at Chicago College of Music.

Appeared as piano soloist with Chicago Symphony Orchestra at the age of nine;

also piano soloist with various other symphony orchestras.

Organized own popular orchestra Chicago 1931, playing larger hotels, night clubs.

Worked in motion picture studios, various capacities since 1937.

Composed and produced, New York theatre, since 1944.

COMPOSER

Motion Picture Scores

Anchor's Aweigh; Tonight And Every Night; Two Guys From Texas; It's A Great Feeling; The Kid From Brooklyn; It Happened In Brooklyn; The West Point Story; My Sister Eileen; Living It Up; Sweater Girl; Priorities 1944.

Motion Picture Title Songs

How To Be Very, Very Popular; Three Coins In The Fountain; All The Way Home; What A Way To Go; Meet Me After The Show

Ballet Scores

Wallflower; Cops and Robbers Ballet for Jerome Robbins

New York Stage Production Scores

High Button Shoes; Gentlemen Prefer Blondes; Two On The Aisle; Hazel Flagg; Peter Pan; Bells Are Ringing; Say, Darling; Gypsy; Do Re Mi; Subways Are For Sleeping; Arturo Ui; Funny Girl; Fade Out Fade In; Darling Of The Day; Hallelujah Baby; Sugar; Lorelei; Gypsy, Revival (Angela Lansbury); Peter Pan, Revival (Sandy Duncan)

Songs

All I Need Is The Girl; As Long As There's Music; Bells Are Ringing; Bye Bye Baby; Can't You Just See Yourself; The Charm Of You; Christmas Waltz; Comes Once In A Lifetime; Conchita Marquita Lopez; Dance Only With Me; Diamonds Are A Girl's Best Friend; Don't Rain On My Parade; Ev'ry Street's A Boulevard In Old New York; Everything's Coming Up Roses; Fade Out Fade In; Five Minutes More; I Give A Little, Get A Little; Guess I'll Hang My Tears Out To Dry; How Do You Speak To An Angel; I Don't Want To Walk Without You, Baby; I Fall In Love Too Easily; I Feel Like I'm Gonna Live Forever; I'll Walk Alone; I Met A Girl; I'm Just Taking My Time; It's Magic; It's The Same Old Dream; It's You Or No One; I've Heard That Song Before; Johnny Freedom; Just A Kiss Apart; Just In Time; Let It Snow, Let It Snow, Let It Snow; Let Me Entertain You; Little Girl From Little Rock; Long Before I Knew You; Make Someone Happy; Never Never Land; On A Sunday By The Sea; Papa, Won't You Dance With Me; The Party's Over; People; Put 'Em In A Box; A Ride On A Rainbow; Saturday Night Is The Loneliest Night In The Week; Say, Darling; Small World; Some People; Stay With The Happy People; Sunday; That's What I Like; There Goes That Song Again; The Things We Did Last Summer; Three Coins In The Fountain; Time After Time; Together Wherever We Go; Victory Polka; Who Are You Now; You Are Woman, I Am Man; You Love Me; You Mustn't Be Discouraged; You're My Girl.

PRODUCER

Theatrical

Pal Joey—Revival

In Any Language (co-producer with George Abbott)

Hazel Flagg

Will Success Spoil Rock Hunter

Mr. Wonderful

Say, Darling

First Impressions

Fade Out—Fade In

Teibele And Her Demon (co-produced with Joe Kipness & Marvin Krauss)

Television

Television Spectacular "Anything Goes"

Best Of Broadway "Panama Hattie"

Peter Pan

Shower Of Stars—Show Stoppers

Eddie Fisher Show

Mr. Magoo's Christmas Carol

The Dangerous Christmas Of Red Riding Hood

The Night The Animals Talked

AWARDS

Composer—Academy Award "Three Coins In The Fountain"

Donaldson Award—"High Button Shoes"

Producer—Donaldson Award "Pal Joey"

Producer—Drama Critics Award "Pal Joey"

Grammy Award—"Gypsy" Cast album

Grammy Award —"Funny Girl"

Tony Award—"Hallelujah Baby"

Songwriter's Hall Of Fame

Jule's Friends At The Palace—Tribute

P R E F A C E

"A word is only as great as the note it sits under"

When Frank Military asked me if I would write the preface to this folio of songs by Jule Styne, I was first flattered and then awed. How to start was the problem.

As a child, Jule Styne was already beginning to display his musical talents to the level of child prodigy. His family migrated from London to Chicago, the spawning ground of such talents as Benny Goodman, Isham Jones, Gus Kahn and many others who started to create what was to become "The Chicago Sound." It wasn't long before Jule Styne, still in his teens, began to play the piano in many of the famed Chicago orchestras, and shortly after wrote his first "hit"—the now standard song called "Sunday" (with another Cahn—spelled Conn). As a pianist of extraordinary accompanying skill, he became one of the most sought after talents for singers. This talent happily brought him to Hollywood where he was under contract to Twentieth Century Fox, coaching and training some of our biggest stars. It was only natural that he would want to create the songs he was coaching rather than just teach them, and he immediately resigned from his high-paying coaching job to accept a much lower salary on the condition that he could write the songs. It wasn't too long before he teamed with Frank Loesser to write the standard classic "I Don't Want To Walk Without You, Baby". Almost at that moment, I was coming to a close of a collaboration with the multi-talented Saul Chaplin, and Sammy Cahn for the first time was "at liberty" and eagerly available when a call came for me to do a film with Jule Styne! I will not intimate that we were successful, I only ask you to turn these pages. I am one of those lyric-writers who says, "A word is only as great as the note it sits under," and Jule Styne has given me and all the "word-people" the greatest notes. I recommend this folio to anyone who loves music—music by Jule Styne!!!

Sammy Cahn
New York, N.Y. '88

Clockwise ▶

Jule at 8— Debut with Chicago Symphony Orchestra

Jule at 18

Jule Styne Family: sister, Claire; mother, Anna; father, Israel; brother, Maury; Jule, age 14

◀ *Top:*
Jule and Sammy Cahn—1943
Phil Silvers and Jule

David Merick, Ethel Merman, Phil Silvers and Jule — "GYPSY"

Jule, Sammy Davis, Jr., and Sandra Church at Stork Club

Frank Sinatra, Jimmy Durante Sammy Cahn Jule Dick Whorf

Jule, Ethel Merman & Richard Nixon Backstage during the original "GYPSY"

◀ *Back Row:* Anthony Quinn, Al Silvani, Barry Sullivan
unknown, Sid Gould, Frank Sinatra, unknown

Front Row: Stanley Styne, unknown, Sammy Cahn,
Jule Styne, Ed Traubner, Hank Sanicola

Jule Styne

◄ *Wife, Margaret and Jule Styne*

Sydney Chaplin, Barbra Streisand, Bob Merrill and Jule

William K. Williams & Jule

Earl Wilson, Jule, Johnny Carson, Joanna Carson, Peter Duchin

Katherine Styne (Daughter) and Jule

Jule Styne

Margaret Whiting, Carol Channing, Jule

Jule, Angela Lansbury, Arthur Laurents, Steve Sondheim

Jule, Barbara Sinatra, Sammy Cahn

Jule, Jerome Robbins

Jule Styne

◀ Top:
Jule and Celeste Holm

Jule & Frank Military

Jule, Betty Comden, Adolph Green

Sammy Cahn & Jule

Standing: Liza Minelli, Sammy Cahn, Earl Wilson, Stanley Adams, Jule
Seated: Marvin Hamlisch & Margaret Styne

Jule Styne

◀ Bottom:
Jule, Adolph Green, Dorothy Dicker—
Jule's manager (A very special thanks
for your help), and Gloria Messenger
(ASCAP)

◀ *Jule and Carol Channing at Jule's 65th Birthday Party.*

Jule, Lee Iacocca, Frank Sinatra

Marvin Hamlisch, Margaret Styne, Nickie Styne, & Jule

Sammy Cahn, Margaret Styne & Jule

Ethel Merman, Arthur Laurents & Jule

Jule Styne

ALL I NEED IS THE GIRL

Words by STEPHEN SONDHEIM
Music by JULE STYNE

Copyright © 1959 by Norbeth Productions, Inc. & Stephen Sondheim
Williamson Music Co. & Stratford Music Corp., owners of the publication and allied rights throughout the World.
International Copyright Secured   ALL RIGHTS RESERVED   Printed in the U.S.A.
Unauthorized copying, arranging, adapting, recording or public performance is an infringement of copyright.
Infringers are liable under the law.

BE A SANTA

Words by BETTY COMDEN, ADOLPH GREEN and JULE STYNE
Music by JULE STYNE

Copyright © 1961 by Betty Comden, Adolph Green and Jule Styne
Stratford Music Corp., owner, Chappell & Co., Inc., Administrator of publication and allied rights for the Western Hemisphere
International Copyright Secured   ALL RIGHTS RESERVED   Printed in the U.S.A.
Unauthorized copying, arranging, adapting, recording or public performance is an infringement of copyright.
Infringers are liable under the law.

AS LONG AS THERE'S MUSIC

Words by SAMMY CAHN
Music by JULE STYNE

The mood be - gins _____ with vi - o - lins _____

And sud - den - ly _____ you're close to me.

Copyright © 1944 by T.B. Harms Company
Copyright Renewed, assigned to Stratford Music Corp.
All rights administered by Chappell & Co., Inc.
International Copyright Secured ALL RIGHTS RESERVED Printed in the U.S.A.
Unauthorized copying, arranging, adapting, recording or public performance is an infringement of copyright.
Infringers are liable under the law.

The tune that they're play - ing _____ is sim - ple and pure; _____

_____ The words keep say - ing that our love will en - dure. _____

Refrain

As long as there's mu - sic _____ and words of ro -

mance, _____ The spell of a theme starts you to

BYE BYE BABY

By LEO ROBIN
and JULE STYNE

© Copyright 1949 (Renewed) by Dorsey Bros. Music, a division of Music Sales Corporation
All Rights Reserved   International Copyright Secured

THE CHARM OF YOU

Words by SAMMY CAHN
Music by JULE STYNE

© 1944 Renewed 1972 METRO-GOLDWYN-MAYER, INC.
Rights Assigned to SBK CATALOGUE PARTNERSHIP, INC.
All Rights Controlled & Administered by SBK FEIST CATALOG, INC.
International Copyright Secured Made in U.S.A. All Rights Reserved
Used by Permission

THE CHRISTMAS WALTZ

Lyric by SAMMY CAHN
Music by JULE STYNE

Copyright © 1954 by Sands Music.
Copyright Renewed, assigned to Producers Music, Inc. (Chappell & Co., Inc., Administrator) and Cahn Music, Inc.
International Copyright Secured ALL RIGHTS RESERVED Printed in the U.S.A.
Unauthorized copying, arranging, adapting, recording or public performance is an infringement of copyright.
Infringers are liable under the law.

CAN'T YOU JUST SEE YOURSELF?

Words by SAMMY CAHN
Music by JULE STYNE

© 1947 EDWIN H. MORRIS & COMPANY, A Division of MPL Communications, Inc.
© Renewed 1975 EDWIN H. MORRIS & COMPANY, A Division of MPL Communications, Inc.
International Copyright Secured   All Rights Reserved

39

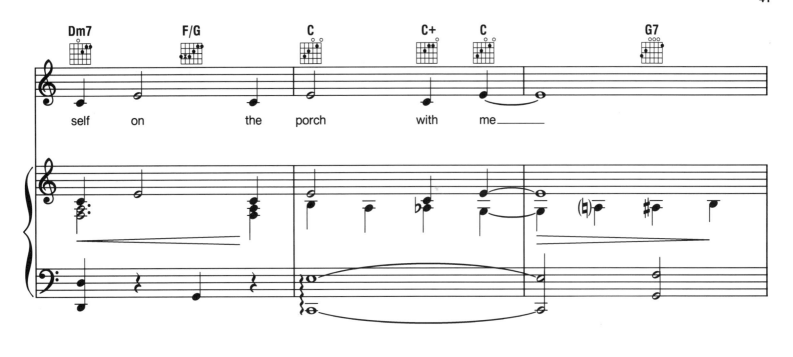

self on the porch with me____

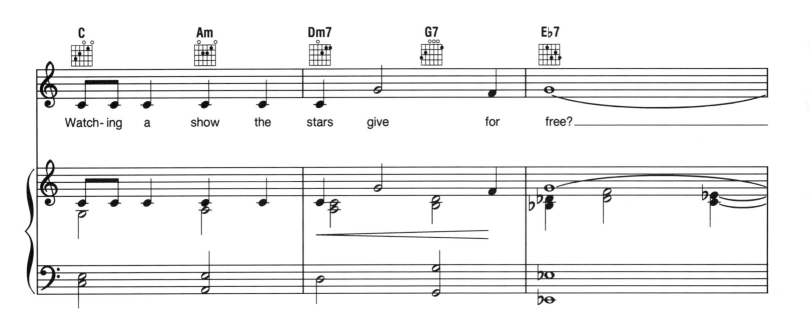

Watch-ing a show the stars give for free?_____

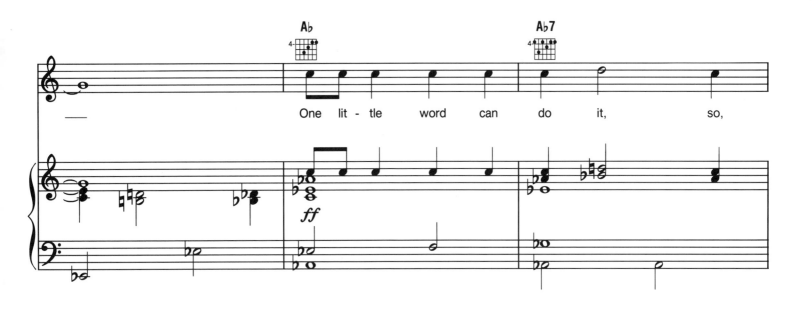

____ One lit-tle word can do it, so,

COME OUT, COME OUT, WHEREVER YOU ARE

Words by SAMMY CAHN
Music by JULE STYNE

Moderato

Copyright © 1944 by Stratford Music Corp. and T.B. Harms
All Rights Controlled by Chappell & Co. and The Welk Music Group
Copyright Renewed
International Copyright Secured ALL RIGHTS RESERVED Printed in the U.S.A.
Unauthorized copying, arranging, adapting, recording or public performance is an infringement of copyright.
Infringers are liable under the law.

Medium Bounce tempo

46

COMES ONCE IN A LIFETIME

Words by BETTY COMDEN and ADOLPH GREEN
Music by JULE STYNE

Copyright © 1961 Betty Comden, Adolph Green and Jule Styne
Stratford Music Corp., owner, Chappell & Co., Inc., Administrator of publication and allied rights for the Western Hemisphere
International Copyright Secured   ALL RIGHTS RESERVED   Printed in the U.S.A.
Unauthorized copying, arranging, adapting, recording or public performance is an infringement of copyright.
Infringers are liable under the law.

DIAMONDS ARE A GIRL'S BEST FRIEND

By LEO ROBIN and JULE STYNE

© Copyright 1949 (Renewed) by Dorsey Bros. Music, a division of Music Sales Corporation
All Rights Reserved   International Copyright Secured

DON'T RAIN ON MY PARADE

(from "FUNNY GIRL")

Words by BOB MERRILL
Music by JULE STYNE

Copyright © 1963 & 1964 by Bob Merrill and Jule Styne
Chappell-Styne, Inc. and Wonderful Music Corp., owners of publication and allied rights throughout the World
Chappell & Co., Inc., sole and exclusive agent
International Copyright Secured ALL RIGHTS RESERVED Printed in the U.S.A.
Unauthorized copying, arranging, adapting, recording or public performance is an infringement of copyright.
Infringers are liable under the law.

55

EV'RY STREET'S A BOULEVARD
(IN OLD NEW YORK)

Words by BOB HILLIARD
Music by JULE STYNE

Copyright © 1953 & 1954 by Jule Styne and Bob Hilliard
Copyright Renewed assigned to Stratford Music Corp. (Chappell & Co., Inc., Administrator) and Better Half Music Co.
International Copyright Secured   ALL RIGHTS RESERVED   Printed in the U.S.A.
Unauthorized copying, arranging, adapting, recording or public performance is an infringement of copyright.
Infringers are liable under the law.

EVERYTHING'S COMING UP ROSES

(from "Gypsy")

Words by STEPHEN SONDHEIM
Music by JULE STYNE

Copyright © 1959 by Norbeth Productions, Inc. and Stephen Sondheim
Williamson Music Co. and Stratford Music Corp. owners of publication and allied rights.
International Copyright Secured ALL RIGHTS RESERVED Printed in the U.S.A.
Unauthorized copying, arranging, adapting, recording or public performance is an infringement of copyright.
Infringers are liable under the law.

FUNNY GIRL

Words by BOB MERRILL
Music by JULE STYNE

Copyright © 1968 by Bob Merrill and Jule Styne
Chappell-Styne, Inc. & Wonderful Music Corp., owners of publication and allied rights throughout the World.
Chappell & Co., Inc., sole selling agent.
International Copyright Secured ALL RIGHTS RESERVED Printed in the U.S.A.
Unauthorized copying, arranging, adapting, recording or public performance is an infringement of copyright.
Infringers are liable under the law.

FIVE MINUTES MORE

Words by SAMMY CAHN
Music by JULE STYNE

© 1946 by MORLEY MUSIC CO., INC.
Copyright Renewed, Assigned to MORLEY MUSIC CO., INC. & CAHN MUSIC COMPANY
All Rights Reserved   Used by Permission

GUESS I'LL HANG MY TEARS OUT TO DRY

Words by SAMMY CAHN
Music by JULE STYNE

Copyright © 1944 by Sammy Cahn and Jule Styne. Copyright Renewed.
Stratford Music Corporation, Publisher and owner of publication and allied rights throughout the world.
Sole selling agent: Chappell & Co., Inc.
International Copyright Secured ALL RIGHTS RESERVED Printed in the U.S.A.
Unauthorized copying, arranging, adapting, recording or public performance is an infringement of copyright.
Infringers are liable under the law.

HOW DO YOU SPEAK TO AN ANGEL?

Words by BOB HILLIARD
Music by JULE STYNE

Copyright © 1952 by Stratford Music Corp. and The Bourne Company
All Rights Controlled by Chappell & Co. and The Bourne Company
Copyright Renewed
International Copyright Secured ALL RIGHTS RESERVED Printed in the U.S.A.
Unauthorized copying, arranging, adapting, recording or public performance is an infringement of copyright.
Infringers are liable under the law.

HEY LOOK, NO CRYIN'

Words by SUSAN BIRKINHEAD
Music by JULE STYNE

Copyright © 1981 by Producers Music Publishing Co., Inc. and Sergeant Music Co.
All Rights Controlled by Chappell & Co. and Sergeant Music Co.
International Copyright Secured   ALL RIGHTS RESERVED   Printed in the U.S.A.
Unauthorized copying, arranging, adapting, recording or public performance is an infringement of copyright.
Infringers are liable under the law.

I BELIEVE

Words by SAMMY CAHN
Music by JULE STYNE

Copyright © 1947 by SINATRA SONGS, INC.
Copyright Renewed, assigned to SANDS MUSIC CORP.
9220 Sunset Blvd., Los Angeles, CA 90069
International Copyright Secured   Made in U.S.A.   All Rights Reserved

I FALL IN LOVE TOO EASILY

Words by SAMMY CAHN
Music by JULE STYNE

There are those who can leave love or take it ___ Love to them is just what they make it ___ I wish that I were the same ___ But love is my fav-'rite game.

© 1944 Renewed 1972 METRO-GOLDWYN-MAYER, INC.
Rights Assigned to SBK CATALOGUE PARTNERSHIP, INC.
All Rights Controlled & Administered by SBK FEIST CATALOG, INC.
International Copyright Secured   Made in U.S.A.   All Rights Reserved
Used by Permission

I STILL GET JEALOUS

Words by SAMMY CAHN
Music by JULE STYNE

© 1947 by MORLEY MUSIC CO., INC.
Copyright Renewed, Assigned to MORLEY MUSIC CO., INC. & CAHN MUSIC COMPANY
All Rights Reserved Used by Permission

I'LL WALK ALONE

Words by SAMMY CAHN
Music by JULE STYNE

© 1944 by MORLEY MUSIC CO., INC.
Copyright Renewed, Assigned to MORLEY MUSIC CO., INC. & CAHN MUSIC COMPANY
All Rights Reserved Used by Permission

I'M GLAD I WAITED FOR YOU

Words by SAMMY CAHN
Music by JULE STYNE

Copyright © 1945 By Shapiro, Bernstein & Co., Inc. New York, NY
Copyright Renewed
International Copyright Secured All Rights Reserved

I'VE HEARD THAT SONG BEFORE

Words by SAMMY CAHN
Music by JULE STYNE

© 1942 by MORLEY MUSIC CO., INC.
Copyright Renewed, Assigned to MORLEY MUSIC CO., INC. & CAHN MUSIC COMPANY
All Rights Reserved Used by Permission

I DON'T WANT TO WALK
WITHOUT YOU BABY

Words by FRANK LOESSER
Music by JULE STYNE

© 1941 (Renewed 1968) PARAMOUNT MUSIC CORP.
All Rights Reserved   Used by Permission

INDIVIDUAL THING

Words by ROBERT MERRILL
Music by JULE STYNE

Copyright © 1971 by VALANDO MUSIC INC. and JULE STYNE
All Rights Controlled by Chappell & Co. and Valando Music Inc.
International Copyright Secured ALL RIGHTS RESERVED Printed in the U.S.A.
Unauthorized copying, arranging, adapting, recording or public performance is an infringement of copyright.
Infringers are liable under the law.

IT'S BEEN A LONG, LONG TIME

Words by SAMMY CAHN
Music by JULE STYNE

© 1945 by MORLEY MUSIC CO., INC.
Copyright Renewed, Assigned to MORLEY MUSIC CO., INC. & CAHN MUSIC COMPANY
All Rights Reserved   Used by Permission

IT'S MAGIC

Words by SAMMY CAHN
Music by JULE STYNE

Copyright © 1948 by M. Witmark & Sons
Copyright renewed, Jule Styne interest assigned to Producer's Music Publishing Co., Inc.
(Administered in the U.S.A. by Chappell & Co., Inc.)
International Copyright Secured ALL RIGHTS RESERVED Printed in the U.S.A.
Unauthorized copying, arranging, adapting, recording or public performance is an infringement of copyright.
Infringers are liable under the law.

IT'S THE SAME OLD DREAM

Words by SAMMY CAHN
Music by JULE STYNE

Copyright © 1947 by SINATRA SONGS, INC.
Copyright Renewed, assigned to SANDS MUSIC CORP.
9220 Sunset Blvd., Los Angeles, CA 90069
International Copyright Secured   Made in U.S.A.   All Rights Reserved

111

KILLING TIME

Words by CAROLYN LEIGH
Music by JULE STYNE

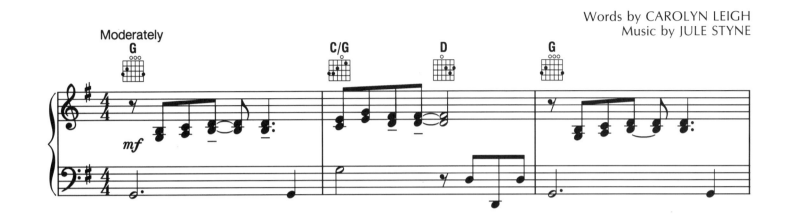

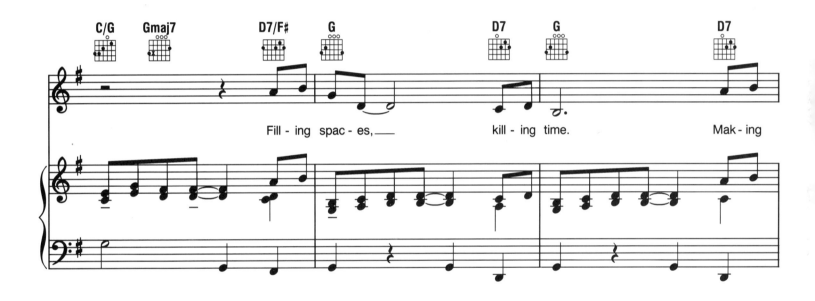

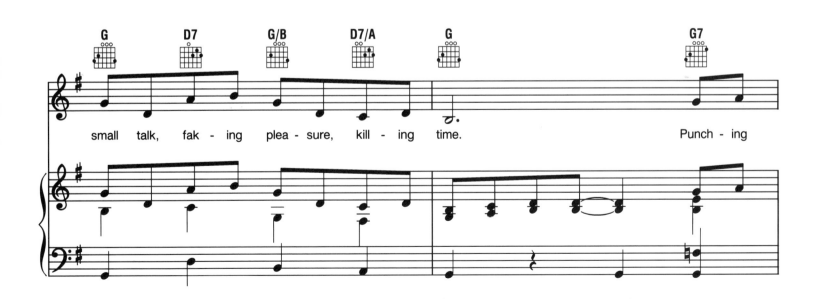

Copyright © 1983 by Producers Music Publishing Company, Inc. and June's Tunes
All Rights Controlled by Chappell & Co. and June's Tunes
International Copyright Secured   ALL RIGHTS RESERVED   Printed in the U.S.A.
Unauthorized copying, arranging, adapting, recording or public performance is an infringement of copyright.
Infringers are liable under the law.

114

IT'S YOU OR NO ONE

Words by SAMMY CAIN
Music by JULE STYNE

Copyright © 1948 By Jule Styne and Warner Bros. Inc.
Copyright Renewed
All Rights Controlled by Chappell & Co. and Warner Bros. Inc.
International Copyright Secured ALL RIGHTS RESERVED Printed in the U.S.A.
Unauthorized copying, arranging, adapting, recording or public performance is an infringement of copyright.
Infringers are liable under the law.

JUST IN TIME
(From "BELLS ARE RINGING")

Words by BETTY COMDEN and ADOLPH GREEN
Music by JULE STYNE

Copyright © 1956 by Betty Comden, Adolph Green word Jule Styne
Copyright Renewed.
Stratford Music Corp., owner, and Chappell & Co., Inc., Administrators of publication and allied rights.
International Copyright Secured   ALL RIGHTS RESERVED   Printed in the U.S.A.
Unauthorized copying, arranging, adapting, recording or public performance is an infringement of copyright.
Infringers are liable under the law.

The los - ing dice were tossed, _____ My bridg - es all were crossed, _____ no - where to go. _____ ___ Now you're here _____ and now I know just where I'm go - ing, no more doubt or fear, _____

LET IT SNOW! LET IT SNOW! LET IT SNOW!

Words by SAMMY CAHN
Music by JULE STYNE

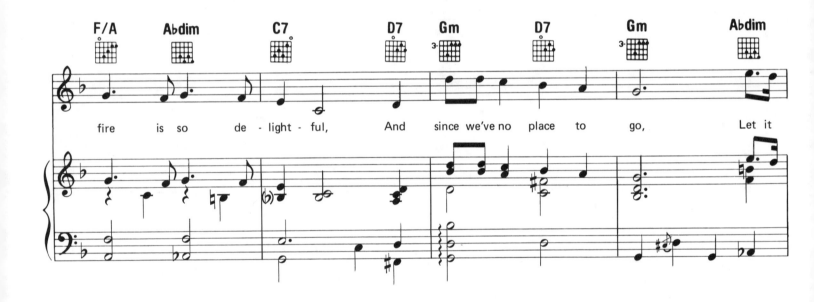

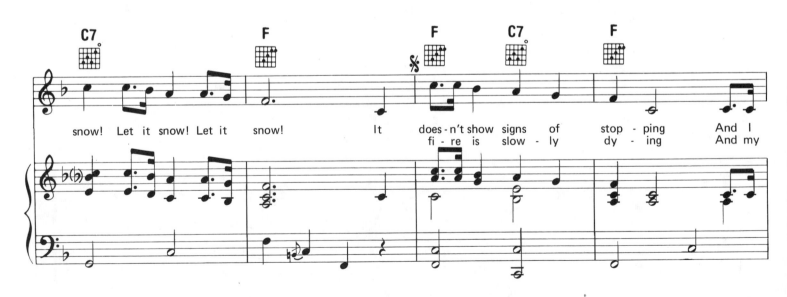

Copyright © 1945 by Jule Styne and Cahn Music Co.
Copyright renewed, Styne interest assigned to Producer's Music Publishing Co., Inc.
(Administered by Chappell & Co., Inc.) for the U.S.A.
International Copyright Secured ALL RIGHTS RESERVED Printed in the U.S.A.
Unauthorized copying, arranging, adapting, recording or public performance is an infringement of copyright.
Infringers are liable under the law.

LET ME ENTERTAIN YOU

Words by STEPHEN SONDHEIM
Music by JULE STYNE

Copyright © 1959 by Norbeth Productions, Inc. and Stephen Sondheim
Williamson Music Co. and Stratford Music Corp., owners of publication and allied rights.
International Copyright Secured ALL RIGHTS RESERVED Printed in the U.S.A.
Unauthorized copying, arranging, adapting, recording or public performance is an infringement of copyright.
Infringers are liable under the law.

old and then some new tricks, I'm ver - y ver - sa - tile.

And if you're real good, I'll make you feel good, I want your spir - its to

climb. Just let me en - ter - tain you, And we'll have a real good

time, yes sir,___ We'll have a real good time.___

LONG BEFORE I KNEW YOU

Words by BETTY COMDEN and ADOLPH GREEN
Music by JULE STYNE

Copyright © 1959 & 1960 by Betty Comden, Adolph Green and Jule Styne
Stratford Music Corp., owner, and Chappell & Co., Inc., Administrators of publication and allied rights for the Western Hemisphere.
International Copyright Secured   ALL RIGHTS RESERVED   Printed in the U.S.A.
Unauthorized copying, arranging, adapting, recording or public performance is an infringement of copyright.
Infringers are liable under the law.

LET'S SEE WHAT HAPPENS

Words by E.Y. HARBURG
Music by by JULE STYNE

Copyright © 1967 by E.Y. Harburg and Jule Styne
All Rights Controlled by Chappell & Co.
International Copyright Secured   ALL RIGHTS RESERVED   Printed in the U.S.A.
Unauthorized copying, arranging, adapting, recording or public performance is an infringement of copyright.
Infringers are liable under the law.

LITTLE GIRL FROM LITTLE ROCK

Words by LEO ROBIN
Music by JULE STYNE

© Copyright 1949 (Renewed) by Dorsey Bros. Music, a division of Music Sales Corporation.
All Rights Reserved International Copyright Secured

135

MAKE SOMEONE HAPPY

Words by BETTY COMDEN and ADOLPH GREEN
Music by JULE STYNE

Copyright © 1960 by Betty Comden, Adolph Green and Jule Styne
Stratford Music Corp., owner, Chappell & Co., Inc., Administrator of publication and allied rights.
International Copyright Secured   ALL RIGHTS RESERVED   Printed in the U.S.A.
Unauthorized copying, arranging, adapting, recording or public performance is an infringement of copyright.
Infringers are liable under the law.

MUSIC THAT MAKES ME DANCE

Words by BOB MERRILL
Music by JULE STYNE

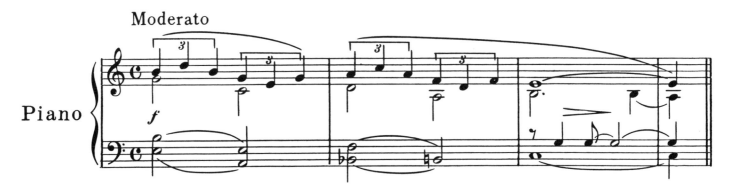

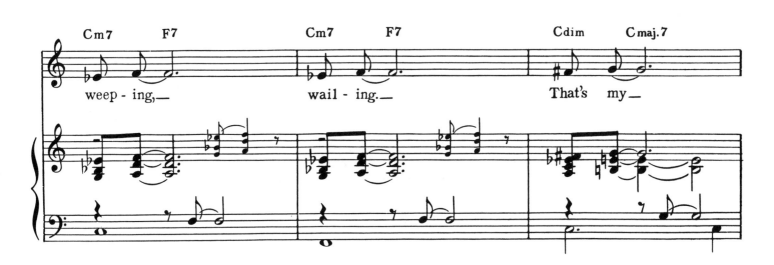

Copyright © 1963 & 1964 by Bob Merrill and Jule Styne
Chappell-Styne, Inc. and Wonderful Music Corp., owners of publication and allied rights.
Chappell & Co., Administrator.
International Copyright Secured ALL RIGHTS RESERVED Printed in the U.S.A.
Unauthorized copying, arranging, adapting, recording or public performance is an infringement of copyright.
Infringers are liable under the law.

Refrain - Expressively with a steady beat

MY OWN MORNING

Words by BETTY COMDEN and ADOLPH GREEN
Music by JULE STYNE

Copyright © 1967 by Betty Comden, Adolph Green and Jule Styne
All Rights Controlled by Stratford Music Corp.
Chappell & Co. Sole Selling Agent
International Copyright Secured ALL RIGHTS RESERVED Printed in the U.S.A.
Unauthorized copying, arranging, adapting, recording or public performance is an infringement of copyright.
Infringers are liable under the law.

NEVER NEVER LAND

Words by BETTY COMDEN and ADOLPH GREEN
Music by JULE STYNE

Moderately

© 1954 BETTY COMDEN, ADOLPH GREEN and JULE STYNE
© Renewed 1982 BETTY COMDEN, ADOLPH GREEN and JULE STYNE
All Rights Throughout the World controlled by EDWIN H. MORRIS & COMPANY, A Division of MPL Communications, Inc.
International Copyright Secured   All Rights Reserved

THE PARTY'S OVER

Words by BETTY COMDEN and ADOLPH GREEN
Music by JULE STYNE

Copyright © 1956 by Betty Comden, Adolph Green and Jule Styne
Copyright Renewed
Stratford Music Corp., Owner, and Chappell & Co., Inc., Administrators of publication and allied rights.
International Copyright Secured   ALL RIGHTS RESERVED Printed in the U.S.A.
Unauthorized copying, arranging, adapting, recording or public performance is an infringement of copyright.
Infringers are liable under the law.

ON A SUNDAY BY THE SEA

Words by SAMMY CAHN
Music by JULE STYNE

*Symbols for Guitar, Diagrams for Ukulele.

Copyright © 1947 by Producers Music Publishing Company and Cahn Music Co.
Copyright Renewed
Producers Music Publishing Company administered by Chappell & Co.
International Copyright Secured ALL RIGHTS RESERVED Printed in the U.S.A.
Unauthorized copying, arranging, adapting, recording or public performance is an infringement of copyright.
Infringers are liable under the law.

PAPA, WON'T YOU DANCE WITH ME?

(From "High Button Shoes")

Words by SAMMY CAHN
Music by JULE STYNE

Copyright © 1947 by Styne and Cahn Music Company, Inc.
Copyright renewed, Styne interest assigned to Producers Music Pub. Co., Inc. (Chappell & Co., Inc., administrator) for the U.S.A.
International Copyright Secured   ALL RIGHTS RESERVED   Printed in the U.S.A.
Unauthorized copying, arranging, adapting, recording, or public performance is an infringement of copyright.
Infringers are liable under the law.

PEOPLE

Words by BOB MERRILL
Music by JULE STYNE

Copyright © 1963 & 1964 by Bob Merrill and Jule Styne
Chappell-Styne, Inc. and Wonderful Music Corp., owners of publication and allied rights .
Chappell & Co., Inc., Administrator
International Copyright Secured ALL RIGHTS RESERVED Printed in the U.S.A.
Unauthorized copying, arranging, adapting, recording or public performance is an infringement of copyright.
Infringers are liable under the law.

A RIDE ON A RAINBOW

Words by LEO ROBIN
Music by JULE STYNE

Copyright © 1957 by Leo Robin and Jule Styne
All Rights Controlled by Chappell & Co.
Copyright Renewed
International Copyright Secured ALL RIGHTS RESERVED Printed in the U.S.A.
Unauthorized copying, arranging, adapting, recording or public performance is an infringement of copyright.
Infringers are liable under the law.

SATURDAY NIGHT IS THE LONELIEST NIGHT OF THE WEEK

Words by SAMMY CAHN
Music by JULE STYNE

Copyright © 1944 by Barton Music, Corp.
Copyright Renewed, Styne interest assigned to Producers Music Publishing Co., Inc. (Chappell & Co., Inc., Administrator) for the U.S.A. only
International Copyright Secured   ALL RIGHTS RESERVED   Printed in the U.S.A.
Unauthorized copying, arranging, adapting, recording or public performance is an infringement of copyright.
Infringers are liable under the law.

170

SMALL WORLD

Words by STEPHEN SONDHEIM
Music by JULE STYNE

Copyright © 1959 by Norbeth Productions, Inc. and Stephen Sondheim
Williamson Music and Stratford Music Corp., owners of publication and allied rights throughout the World.
International Copyright Secured   ALL RIGHTS RESERVED   Printed in the U.S.A.
Unauthorized copying, arranging, adapting, recording or public performance is an infringement of copyright.
Infringers are liable under the law.

SOME OTHER TIME

Words by SAMMY CAHN
Music by JULES STYNE

Copyright © 1944 by Stratford Music Corp. and T.B. Harms
All Rights Controlled by Chappell & Co. and The Welk Music Group
Copyright Renewed
International Copyright Secured   ALL RIGHTS RESERVED   Printed in the U.S.A.
Unauthorized copying, arranging, adapting, recording or public performance is an infringement of copyright.
Infringers are liable under the law.

Chorus
Slowly with expression

(Doin' It For)
SUGAR

Words by BOB MERRILL
Music by JULE STYNE

Copyright © 1972 by Bob Merrill and Jule Styne
Chappell & Co., Inc. and Merrill Music Corp. owners of publication and allied rights throughout the world.
International Copyright Secured ALL RIGHTS RESERVED Printed in the U.S.A.
Unauthorized copying, arranging, adapting, recording or public performance is an infringement of copyright.
Infringers are liable under the law.

SOME PEOPLE

Words by STEPHEN SONDHEIM
Music by JULE STYNE

Copyright © 1959 by Norbeth Productions, Inc. and Stephen Sondheim
Williamson Music Co. and Stratford Music Corp., owners of publication and allied rights throughout the world.
International Copyright Secured   ALL RIGHTS RESERVED Printed in the U.S.A.
Unauthorized copying, arranging, adapting, recording or public performance is an infringement of copyright.
Infringers are liable under the law.

THE THINGS WE DID LAST SUMMER

Words and Music by SAMMY CAHN
and JULE STYNE

Copyright © 1946 by Edwin H. Morris & Co., Inc.
Copyright renewed, assigned to Producer's Music Publishing Co., Inc.
(Chappell & Co., Inc., administrator) and Cahn Music Co. for the U.S.A. only
International Copyright Secured ALL RIGHTS RESERVED Printed in the U.S.A.
Unauthorized copying, arranging, adapting, recording or public performance is an infringement of copyright.
Infringers are liable under the law.

THREE COINS IN THE FOUNTAIN

Words by SAMMY CAHN
Music by JULE STYNE

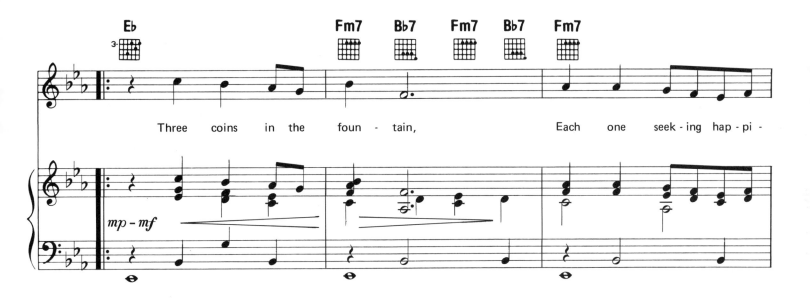

Three coins in the foun - tain, Each one seek - ing hap - pi -

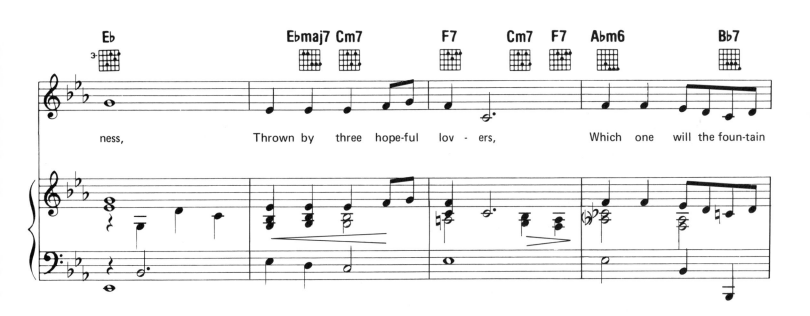

ness, Thrown by three hope-ful lov - ers, Which one will the foun-tain

Copyright © 1954 by Robbins Music Corporation
Copyright renewed, Styne interest assigned to Producer's Music Publishing Co., Inc.
(Chappell & Co., Inc., administrator) for the U.S.A. and Canada
International Copyright Secured ALL RIGHTS RESERVED Printed in the U.S.A.
Unauthorized copying, arranging, adapting, recording or public performance is an infringement of copyright.
Infringers are liable under the law.

TIME AFTER TIME

Words by SAMMY CAHN
Music by JULE STYNE

Copyright © 1947 by SINATRA SONGS, INC.
Copyright Renewed, assigned to SANDS MUSIC CORP.
9220 Sunset Blvd., Los Angeles, CA 90069
International Copyright Secured   Made in U.S.A.   All Rights Reserved

TO A SMALL DEGREE

Words by ROBERT MERRILL
Music by JULE STYNE

Copyright © 1971 by VALANDO MUSIC INC. and JULE STYNE
All Rights Controlled by Chappell & Co. and Valando Music Inc.
International Copyright Secured ALL RIGHTS RESERVED Printed in the U.S.A.
Unauthorized copying, arranging, adapting, recording or public performance is an infringement of copyright.
Infringers are liable under the law.

WHO ARE YOU NOW

Words by BOB MERRILL
Music by JULE STYNE

Copyright © 1963 & 1964 by Bob Merrill and Jule Styne
Chappell-Styne, Inc. and Wonderful Music Corp., owners of publication and allied rights.
Chappell & CO., Administrator.
International Copyright Secured ALL RIGHTS RESERVED Printed in the U.S.A.
Unauthorized copying, arranging, adapting, recording or public performance is an infringement of copyright.
Infringers are liable under the law.

TOGETHER WHEREVER WE GO

Words by STEPHEN SONDHEIM
Music by JULE STYNE

Copyright © 1959 by Norbeth Productions, Inc. and Stephen Sondheim
Williamson Music Co. and Stratford Music Corp., owners of publication and allied rights.
International Copyright Secured   ALL RIGHTS RESERVED   Printed in the U.S.A.
Unauthorized copying, arranging, adapting, recording or public performance is an infringement of copyright.
Infringers are liable under the law.

209

WHAT MAKES THE SUNSET

Words by SAMMY CAHN
Music by JULE STYNE

© 1944 Renewed 1977 METRO-GOLDWYN-MAYER, INC.
Rights Assigned to SBK CATALOGUE PARTNERSHIP, INC.
All Rights Controlled & Administered by SBK MILLER CATALOG, INC.
International Copyright Secured   Made in U.S.A.   All Rights Reserved
Used by Permission

YOU'LL NEVER GET AWAY FROM ME

Words by STEPHEN SONDHEIM
Music by JULE STYNE

Copyright © 1959 by Norbeth Productions, Inc. and Stephen Sondheim
All Rights Controlled by Williamson Music Company and Stratford Music Corp. (Administered by Chappell & Co.)
International Copyright Secured ALL RIGHTS RESERVED Printed in the U.S.A.
Unauthorized copying, arranging, adapting, recording or public performance is an infringement of copyright.
Infringers are liable under the law.

you could say "Hey, here's your hat," But a lit - tle

thing like that could - n't stop me now.

I could - n't get a -

way from you E - ven if you told me to,

YOU'RE MY GIRL

Music by JULE STYNE
Lyrics by SAMMY CAHN

Copyright © 1947 by Styne and Cahn Music Company, Inc.
Copyright renewed, Styne interest assigned to Producer's Music Publishing Co., Inc.
(Chappell & Co., Inc., Administrator) for the United States
International Copyright Secured ALL RIGHTS RESERVED Printed in the U.S.A.
Unauthorized copying, arranging, adapting, recording or public performance is an infringement of copyright.
Infringers are liable under the law.

YOU ARE WOMAN, I AM MAN

Words by BOB MERRILL
Music by JULE STYNE

Moderately

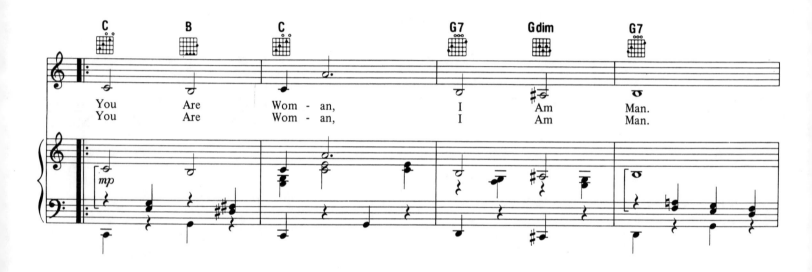

You Are Wom-an, I Am Man.
You Are Wom-an, I Am Man.

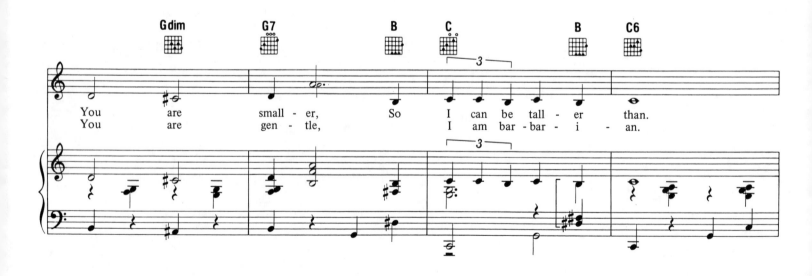

You are small-er, So I can be tall-er than.
You are gen-tle, I am bar-bar-i-an.

Copyright © 1963 & 1964 by Bob Merrill and Jule Styne
Chappell-Styne, Inc. and Wonderful Music Corp., owners of publication and allied rights throughout the World.
Chappell & Co., Inc., sole selling agent
International Copyright Secured ALL RIGHTS RESERVED Printed in the U.S.A.
Unauthorized copying, arranging, adapting, recording or public performance is an infringement of copyright.
Infringers are liable under the law.